40 DAYS THROUGH THE BOOK

COLOSSIANS

ONE JESUS, ONE PEOPLE

STUDY GUIDE | 6 SESSIONS

JAY Y. KIM

WITH KEVIN AND SHERRY HARNEY

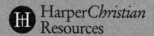

HarperChristian Resources

40 Days Through the Book: Colossians
© 2022 by Jay Y. Kim

Requests for information should be addressed to: HarperChristian Resources, 3900 Sparks Dr. SE, Grand Rapids, Michigan 49546

ISBN 978-0-310-14827-2 (softcover)
ISBN 978-0-310-14828-9 (ebook)

HarperChristian Resources titles may be purchased in bulk for church, business, fundraising, or ministry use. For information, please e-mail ResourceSpecialist@ChurchSource.com.

The themes of this study are drawn from the video study of the same name by Jay Y. Kim. All other resources, including the session introductions, small group discussion questions, prayer direction, and the 40 Days learning and reflection exercises and have been written by Kevin and Sherry Harney in collaboration with Jay Y. Kim.

First printing August 2022 / Printed in the United States of America

CONTENTS

HOW TO USE THIS GUIDE

SCOPE AND SEQUENCE

Welcome to the *40 Days Through the Book* study on Colossians! During the course of the next six weeks, you and your fellow group members will embark on an in-depth exploration of Paul's message to this church in Colossae. During this study, you will learn when he wrote the book, approximately when it was written, and the background and context in which it was written. But, more importantly, through the teaching by Jay Y. Kim, you will explore the key themes that Paul relates in the book—and how his teachings apply to you today.

SESSION OUTLINE

The *40 Days Through the Book* video and study guide are designed to be experienced both in group settings (such as a Bible study, Sunday school class, or small group gatherings) as well as in your individual study time. Each session begins with an introductory reading and question. You will then watch the video message. (Play the DVD or refer to the instructions on the inside front cover on how to access the sessions at any time through streaming.) An outline has been provided in the guide for you to take notes and gather your reflections as you watch the video. Next, if you are doing this study with a group, you will engage in a time of directed discussion, review the memory verses for the week, and close with a time of prayer. (Note that if your group is larger, you may wish to watch the videos together and then break into smaller groups of four to six people, to ensure that everyone has time to participate in discussions.)

40-DAY JOURNEY

What is truly unique about this study, and all of the other studies in the *40 Days Through the Book* series, are the daily learning resources that will lead you into a deeper engagement with the text. Each week, you will be given a set of daily readings, with accompanying reflection questions, to help you explore the material that you covered during your group time.

The first day's reading will focus on the key verse to memorize for the week. In the other weekly readings, you will be invited to read a passage from Colossians, reflect on the text, and then respond with some guided journal questions. On the final day, you will review the key verse again and recite it from memory. As you work through the six weeks' worth of material in this section, you will read (and, in some cases, reread) the entire book of Colossians.

Now, you may be wondering why you will be doing this over the course of *forty* days. Certainly, there is nothing special about that number. But there is something biblical about it. In the Bible, the number forty typically designates a time of *testing*. Noah was in the ark for forty days. Moses lived forty years in Egypt and another forty years in the desert before he led God's people. He spent forty days on Mount Sinai receiving God's laws and sent spies, for forty days, to investigate the land of Canaan. Later, God sent the prophet Jonah to warn ancient Nineveh, for forty days, that its destruction would come because of the people's sins.

Even more critically, in the New Testament we read that Jesus spent forty days in the wilderness, fasting and praying. It marked a critical transition point in his ministry—the place where he set about to fulfill the mission that God had intended. During this time Jesus was tested relentlessly by the enemy . . . and prevailed. When he returned to Galilee, he was a different person than the man who had entered into the wilderness forty days before. The same will be true for you as you commit to this forty-day journey through Colossians.

GROUP FACILITATION

If you are doing this study with a group, everyone should have a copy of this study guide. Not only will this help you engage when your group is meeting, but it will also allow you to fully enter into the *40 Days* learning experience. Keep in mind the video, questions, and activities are simply tools to help you engage with the session. The real power and life-transformation will come as you dig into the Scriptures and seek to live out the truths you learn along the way.

Finally, you will need to appoint a leader or facilitator for the group who is responsible for starting the video teaching and for keeping track of time during discussions and activities. Leaders may also read questions aloud and monitor discussions, prompting participants to respond and ensuring that everyone has the opportunity to participate. For more thorough instructions on this role, see the Leader's Guide included at the back of this guide.

INTRODUCTION

COLOSSIANS

AUTHOR, DATE, AND LOCATION

Some of the apostle Paul's letters were written to believers who lived in cultural centers like Rome, Thessalonica, and Ephesus. The letter to the Colossians was different. It was sent to the southeast region of what is now known as Turkey. This was *not* a major trade center. It was *not* a hub of culture. The Colossian Christians lived in a place of moderate importance. It was a town much like where most people live around the world today. Jews and Gentiles lived side by side. There was ethnic and religious diversity. Judaism, Christianity, local religions and emperor worship each offered their own unique sets of values and beliefs. Sometime between 60 and 62 AD, the apostle Paul wrote to these early Christians who found themselves floundering amidst the muddled mishmash of religious syncretism. The simple message of the gospel of Jesus had become contaminated with injections of cultural beliefs and false religions. Paul wrote to remind them there is just one Jesus and one Church.

THE BIG PICTURE

In the first century, polytheism was the norm. There were many religions and countless expressions of faith. Temples built for a vast variety of gods dotted the landscape of almost every city and small town. One time, when the apostle Paul was in the city of Athens, he noticed all the places of worship. There was even an altar with the inscription, "TO AN UNKNOWN GOD" (Acts 17:23). These people were so attentive to the pantheon of false gods that they made a place for any god they had missed or forgotten. Paul used this as a chance to point them to Jesus, Emmanuel, the one true God who came to live among us.

The book of Colossians, made up of just four short chapters, is massive when it comes to powerful teaching on the person of Jesus. Colossians 1:15–20 is one of the most concise and pointed declarations of the uniqueness of Jesus and divinity of our Lord in all the Bible. There is just one Jesus and when we know who he is, we have clear direction for our beliefs and life. If we water down the person of Jesus or add false religious or cultural beliefs, he is no longer the one Jesus. Paul was writing to correct the heretical teaching that was swirling around the church in Colossae.

Another massive challenge that existed in the first century was division among people. Like at all times in history, and in every part of the world, people can be divided because of ethnicity, gender, social class, religion, and a massive list of other things. The apostle Paul is addressing this problem among the Colossian believers. The world might be divided over these things, but Christians should not be. When Jesus is at the center of our hearts, lives, homes, churches, and community life, we are made one. Believers can say with bold confidence, "We are one people," even when we have diverse backgrounds and differing views.

Paul's central message to the Colossian believers is that we worship one Jesus and are part of one people (the Church). He goes on to expound this reality by presenting clear beliefs and theology in the first two chapters. It is right thinking that moves us toward Jesus and each other. In chapters three and four Paul turns our attention to right living that grows out of our beliefs. When we live according to the teachings and ways of Jesus, the world will see that we worship one Jesus as a unified people of God.

EPIC THEMES

There are many themes in Colossians that are worthy of our focus. Some of these include:

- **There is power in prayer**. Believers pray for each other with thankful hearts. We show our unity as we ask God to help other Christians know God, live for him, bear fruit, live in power, and walk in joy (see Colossians 1:1–14).

- **There is one Jesus, and he is the true center.** The world might bow and worship idols, emperors, and false gods, but Jesus alone is Lord and worthy of praise (see Colossians 1:15–23).

- **Jesus sets us free from the bondage of legalism and human traditions.** The world and religious traditionalism can lead to bondage and emptiness. Jesus comes to give us roots and strengthen us so that we are not lured into false religion (see Colossians 1:21–2:15).

- **Reality is not found in religion but in a relationship with Jesus and his people.** There is a tendency to grasp for straws and shadows. Jesus is real, solid, and the rock on which we build our faith and life. Christians find their reality in Jesus alone and reject cheap imitations (see Colossians 2:16–23).

- **There is a battle we all face.** The enticements of sin invite us all to wander from Jesus and embrace the glittery and attractive things of the world. The resurrection of Jesus and his presence with us should move us from the things of the world and right into the arms of our Savior, over and over again (see Colossians 3:1–11).

- **God offers new "clothes."** When we come to faith in Jesus, we are called to put off our old ways, attitudes, actions . . . the clothes of the past. At the same time, we are moved to dress ourselves in the things of Jesus . . . a whole new lifestyle that fits who we are as children of God (see Colossians 3:12–4:1).

- **We share the mystery of Christ.** When we learn there is one Jesus and stand united as one people, we are moved to proclaim this life-transforming mystery of the gospel to all who will listen (see Colossians 4:2–18).

The world has always been divided. Conflict seems to be hard-wired into the broken hearts and minds of sinful human beings. In Christ we find unity in the one Jesus who rules and reigns over our hearts, the Church, and the world. As Christians live in unity as one people, we set an example for the world. Peace is possible. Conflict does not have to go on endlessly. God's people can love each other even when we face the same things that seem to divide people in our world. What an opportunity to show the world that unity is possible for those who know, love, and follow Jesus!

THE TRUE CENTER

COLOSSIANS 1:1–29

There is a human tendency to place ourselves at the center of our own little universe. With piercingly beautiful words and Spirit-inspired clarity, the apostle Paul declares that there is only one center around which a faithful Christian can orbit and not have life spin out of control. Jesus, the divine One, is our center.

WELCOME

Big, bold, brash claims! We have all heard them. Muhamad Ali, the great boxer known for his success in the ring and his equally effective verbal jabs outside the ring declared things like, "I float like a butterfly and sting like a bee!" He also claimed to be, "The greatest of all time!"

Decades later another sports story has been unfolding as people debate who is the best basketball player in history. Should the title go to Michael "Air" Jordan or LeBron "King" James? Who is the greatest basketball player to ever grace the courts of the NBA? Lots of people have claimed that Lebron James is the G.O.A.T! And lots of other people are equally sure that Michael Jordan is the **Greatest Of All Time**! The battle and debate rages on.

In the days of Jesus and the early Church, there was a procession of Roman emperors who claimed to be the divine center of the empire. One by one, they passed from this life and into history. Over time, it was clear that their claims were radically overstated and anyone who made these human leaders the center of their life had missed the mark.

More than 2,000 years ago, an itinerant rabbi with no home, no political influence, and no formal religious organization claimed to be "the way, the truth and the life" (John 14:6). On one occasion, this wandering teacher invoked the divine name of God when he spoke to Moses at the burning bush (see Exodus 3:14; John 8:58). The religious leaders of the day were so convinced that Jesus was claiming to be God, and the single way to eternal life with the Father, they had him nailed to a Roman cross. They delighted as his blood poured to the ground and his life was snuffed out after only thirty-three years walking on this earth. When Jesus declared he was the divine center of all things, he made the boldest claim in the history of the world.

For more than 2,000 years his followers have worshiped Jesus as their Lord and sought to place him at the center of their lives, homes, churches, and even their culture. Two millennia after the incarnation, life, death, resurrection, and ascension of Jesus, more than 2.3 billion people practice some form of faith based on the teaching and life of this one man.

Though persecution of Christians continues and even grows in many parts of the world, Jesus is still Lord of all. Although secular philosophies blossom and thrive, Jesus is risen, alive, and invites every person to receive his grace and leadership.

The question is not, "Is Jesus the true center of all things?" He is!

The real question is, "Will I let him be the center of my life today and every day?"

SHARE

Tell about a time on your journey with Jesus when he was at the center of your attention, heart, and life. How did this impact the way you lived, loved, and labored in that season?

WATCH

Watch the video segment for session one. (Play the DVD or see the instructions on the inside front cover on how to access the sessions through streaming.) As you watch, use the following outline to record any thoughts or concepts that stand out to you.

What is at the center?

Who is at the center? (John 14:6)?

The context and setting of Colossians (Colossians 1:1–5)

Syncretism and false teaching in the Church. . . . then and now (Colossians 1:5; Philippians 3:20)

The primary reason for the letter to the Colossian church . . . course correction

The danger of *materialism*

The seduction of *individualism*

The lure of *nationalism*

Who is at the center—me or Jesus? (Colossians 1:15–20)

Was Jesus . . .

Deceived?

Deluded?

Divine?

The importance and role of the firstborn in the ancient world
(Colossians 1:15)

Opening our eyes to recognize the temptation of syncretism
and fixing our eyes on Jesus, the true center of it all!

DISCUSS

Take a few minutes with your group members to discuss what
you just watched and explore these concepts in Scripture. Use
the following questions to help guide your discussion.

I. What impacted you the most as you watched Jay's teaching?

2. The church in Colossae was facing the temptation to embrace syncretistic beliefs and practices. They were enticed to combine the current cultural and religious beliefs, values, and practices with their Christian faith. How are Christians today facing the temptation to fuse *one* of these "isms" with their faith in Jesus?

   ◦ Materialism
   ◦ Individualism
   ◦ Nationalism
   ◦ Some other "ism"

3. **Read Colossians 1:3–6.** The apostle Paul emphasizes "the true message of the gospel." When you let any "ism," belief system, or personal preference influence your faith in Jesus, things become murky and diluted, and your faith gets watered down. Describe a time you saw this happen in your life or the faith journey or someone you know. Why is this so dangerous that the apostle Paul warns you about it?

4. **Read Colossians 1:15–20.** Make a list of the things this passage declares about Jesus. What are the implications for the Church and your life of faith if each one is true?

5. When you understand that Jesus is the firstborn and live with him as your true center (both in community with God's people and in your individual faith journey), what impact can this have on *one* of the areas below?

   - How you deal with the enticement to sin and wander from God's care
   - How you relate to other followers of Jesus in your church and community
   - When you face times of darkness and pain
   - How you relate to people who are far from Jesus or antagonistic to your faith
   - How you care for and relate to members of your family
   - Some other area or aspect of your life

6. What is a specific way you have learned to slow down and fix your eyes on Jesus in the busyness of life and the storms you face? How has this practice helped you keep Jesus in the center of your life?

MEMORIZE

At each session, you will be given a key verse (or verses) from the passage covered in the video teaching to memorize. This week, your memory verses are from Colossians 1:19–20:

> *For God was pleased to have all his fullness dwell in him, and through him to reconcile to himself all things, whether things on earth or things in heaven, by making peace through his blood, shed on the cross.*

Have everyone recite these verses out loud. Then go around the room and ask for any volunteers who would like to say the verses from memory.

RESPOND

What will you take away from this session? What is one practical next step you can take to fix your eyes on Jesus as the center of your life, community, and the world?

PRAY

Close your group time by praying in any of the following directions:

- Praise, worship, and celebrate Jesus as the divine center of the universe, your church, and your life.
- Pray for churches, other believers, and yourself to recognize when syncretism is slipping into our thinking and practices. Ask for the power of the Holy Spirit to resist this deceptive temptation.
- Confess where you have let any sort of "ism" or syncretistic thinking taint your purity of faith in Jesus alone. (You might want to do this as a group or make time for silent confession.)
- Lift up members of your group and pray that they will follow, worship, and live for Jesus as the true and only center of their life.

SESSION ONE

Reflect on the material you have covered in this session by engaging in the following between-session learning resources. Each week, you will begin by reviewing the key verse(s) to memorize for the session. During the next five days, you will have an opportunity to read a portion of Colossians, reflect on what you learn, respond by taking action, journal some of your insights, and pray about what God has taught you. Finally, on the last day, you will review the theme of the session, reflect on what you have learned, and review how it has impacted your life.

DAY 1

Memorize: Begin this week's personal study by reciting Colossians 1:19–20:

> *For God was pleased to have all his fullness dwell in him, and through him to reconcile to himself all things, whether things on earth or things in heaven, by making peace through his blood, shed on the cross.*

Now try to say these verses completely from memory.

Reflect: All of the fulness of divinity dwells in Jesus. He is God with us. The center of all things. Jesus is in the reconciliation business. We know that he came to reconcile us to the Father through his sacrifice, but there is much more. Stop and ponder this truth: Jesus came to reconcile everything in heaven and on the earth to himself. Let that reality wash over your soul and fill your mind. What is Jesus presently healing, restoring, and reconciling in your life? What is he restoring and reconciling in the world around us? How can you rejoice in the reconciling work of Jesus?

DAY 2

Read: Colossians 1:1-2.

Reflect: The Holy Spirit inspired the apostle Paul to write to "brothers and sisters" in Christ in the city of Colossae. So often we read the Bible in isolation and filter it through our own mind, life, and immediate needs. There is no question that the Scriptures relate to each believer and that God wants to speak to you personally. But there is something bigger going on here. God is building a church made up of people from every tribe and nation. As you read the Bible, listen with ears and a heart as big as the vision of God. Our Savior came to offer himself for people from every walk of life. Read his Word with the whole human family in mind and you will receive fresh perspectives and vistas you have never seen before. How do I tend to read the Bible? Who do I think God is speaking to?

Journal:
- How can you expand you understanding of the Scriptures by reading (or listening) with a larger audience in mind?
- How might your life change if you learned from the Scriptures in a community (like your small group and in church services) and let the presence and insights of other people help shape your faith in Jesus?

Pray: Pray for your group members by name and ask God to grow each of them as they open God's Word and learn from the teaching of the Bible.

DAY 3

Read: Colossians 1:3–8.

Reflect: Praying for God's people is a central theme in the Bible. In this passage we are captured by the heart and spirit of prayer. Paul and his ministry partners are "always thankful." What a beautiful picture! They have heard about the growing faith, the unquenchable hope, and expansive love of the Colossian Christians. These people are fruitful in sharing the good news of Jesus and they live in the grace of God. Do you get a sense that Paul knows and loves these people (if even from a distance)? He and his companions are praying often with hearts filled with joy. Who do you pray for in your church and in other churches? What is your knowledge of the spiritual condition of these people? How can you pray with increasing passion and frequency?

Journal:
- How can you get to know the spiritual condition of other believers in greater depth?
- How can you increase your passion and engagement in praying for other Christians in your church and in other churches in the community where you live?

Pray: Think about two or three other churches in your community that worship and follow Jesus as the Lord of the universe and center of their congregation. Pray for these churches with a thankful heart, asking for God to grow their faith, hope, and love.

DAY 4

Read: Colossians 1:9–14.

Reflect: In Colossians 1:3–8 we are captured by the spirit and heart of Paul's prayer for the church. In this passage we are stunned by the powerful content of his prayer. Reflect on what the apostle and his ministry colleagues are praying for these believers and learn from their example. They are praying for:

- Knowledge of God's will . . .
- Power to live a life worthy of the Lord . . .
- Strength to live in ways that please God . . .
- To bear fruit in all they do . . .
- Growth in the knowledge of God . . .
- The believers to be strengthened and empowered . . .
- To live with great endurance and patience . . .
- The Colossian Christians to share in the inheritance of God's people . . .

If you have ever been praying for another believer and wondered what to lift up to heaven on their behalf, Colossians 1:9–14 is a great place to start. What do you learn about the content of prayer for other Christians in this passage?

Journal:

- Write down the names of three Christians you love and care about. How could you pray the content of this prayer for each one of these people?
- What might happen if you begin praying the content of this passage for yourself? What might God do in you as the power of heaven is unleashed?

Pray: Take time right now and pray each theme of this prayer for yourself and for one other Christian you love and care about.

DAY 5

Read: Colossians 1:15–20.

Reflect: This passage expresses, with laser-like precision, the person of Jesus. You could spend an hour reflecting on this passage every day for a year and still not comprehend the greatness of the sovereign Lord of the universe. The closing words point us to a hill called "the skull" and to a Savior whose body was broken and whose blood was poured out for our salvation. The pinnacle of this passage points not to heaven but to a place on this planet where the divine One bore the shame that broken and rebellious people deserved. From the stench of a stable to the torture of Roman execution, the life of Jesus was marked by sacrifice. Our reconciliation was bought at an infinite price as the center of the universe moved into our space, time, and skin. This rich passage focuses on Jesus, the Lord of glory. Why do you think it begins with Jesus' power, creation, glory, sovereignty, and supremacy but ends with sacrifice, blood, and a cross?

Journal:
- What do you learn about Jesus in this passage?
- What does each thing you learn about Jesus teach you about yourself?

Pray: Take this passage and personalize it into a prayer lifted up directly to Jesus. Jesus, you are the Son of God, the perfect image of the God I can't see. You are the firstborn of all creation. . . .

DAY 6

Read: Colossians 1:21–29.

Reflect: When we recognize the magnitude of and reason for Jesus' suffering, we hear the Spirit of God invite us to join him on this journey of sacrifice. Paul actually tells the Colossian believers that he rejoices that he is able to suffer in his service to the Church, including their congregation. For the sake of God's people, the body of Christ, Paul is willing to bear physical pain in his own body. What a picture! What a declaration! Paul has been transformed from a powerful and aggressive persecutor of the Church to a humble servant who is honored to suffer for God's people. When Paul sees the hope of the glory of Jesus come alive in other people, both Jewish and Gentile, he is willing to pay any price. This is one picture of what it means to become like the Savior. What are you willing to sacrifice and give up for the sake of Jesus and to help others come and receive the hope of glory?

Journal:
- Reflect on people who sacrificed and even suffered to share the truth and grace of Jesus with you. What could you do to honor, thank, or encourage these people?

- What are one or two ways you could count the cost, sacrifice, or suffer for the sake of following Jesus?

Pray: Thank Jesus for the people who willingly and gladly sacrificed so that you could come to know Jesus, the hope of glory. Pray that you will have this kind of impact on the lives of many others.

DAY 7

Memorize: Conclude this week's personal study by again reciting Colossians 1:19–20:

> *For God was pleased to have all his fullness dwell in him, and through him to reconcile to himself all things, whether things on earth or things in heaven, by making peace through his blood, shed on the cross.*

Now try to say these verses completely from memory.

Reflect: Peace through sacrifice. Jesus came to heal our relationship with the Father in heaven and to allow us to love each other and live for him. This peace comes through his life, death, and resurrection. It was sealed by his blood shed for us. How has the finished work of Jesus on the cross brought peace in your life, relationships, and with God? Is there a relationship where you are not living in peace? How can you bring this to Jesus and ask for his completed work to empower you to seek restoration, reconciliation, or peace in this relationship?

BROKEN GAUGES

COLOSSIANS 2:1–15

When a warning gauge on the dashboard of a car or on a high-power machine is not working, the question is not, will things blow up? The real question is, when will things explode? The same is true in our spiritual lives. When we use the broken gauges and measurements of the world rather than Christ, we are headed for disaster. But when we are rooted, built up, and strengthened in Christ, we can walk in confident hope.

WELCOME

Where do you put your trust? In a world with ever-increasing suspicion and doubt, many people are growing skeptical of almost everything. The conduits of communication and cultural gauges that have guided people are no longer looked at as dependable.

For years professional pollsters have done research and shared their insights and many people have accepted their results as a fair reflection of the cultural climate. News anchors showed up on TV every evening at a prescribed time and people of diverse political views listened and had an implicit confidence that what these people said was researched and real. Doctors gave their prescriptions and advice and patients walked away certain of the best course of action. Pastors stood in pulpits and taught from the Bible and congregational members believed they had heard words from God and the Word of God.

Now, polls are suspect. News is ever-present and often questioned. Doctors still give prescriptions and medical advice but many people listen with tainted skepticism. Pastors still preach but built-in trust has been eroded and needs to be earned again and again. The world has changed.

Can we trust the gauges we have used in the past? Should we have trusted these gauges back then? Do we recognize that human standards and structures are always faulty? Maybe there is wisdom in questioning the gauges and guidelines offered to us by our culture.

What if God loves his children so much that he offers clear and trustworthy direction for every aspect of our lives? Perhaps the Maker of Heaven has established gauges and guidelines that don't change with the winds of culture. Maybe the wise Creator who spoke all things into existence can offer us a source of truth that leads to trustful confidence in our increasingly suspicious world.

How do we respond when the gauges we rely on begin to break and things start to overheat and get messy? We look to the one Lord and Savior who wants the best for us and whose words of truth can be trusted. He also gives us himself, the very Word of heaven that brings hope, stability, and confidence in our uncertain world.

SHARE

Tell about a time you trusted something you read, heard, or were told only to find out you were not given the truth (or the whole truth). What price did you pay for being overly trusting?

WATCH

Watch the video segment for session two. (Play the DVD or see the instructions on the inside front cover on how to access the sessions through streaming.) As you watch, use the following outline to record any thoughts or concepts that stand out to you.

The battle between fullness in Christ and living on empty (Colossians 2:1–4)

The source of true wisdom and knowledge (Colossians 2:3)

Stop spinning your wheels

Christ rules and reigns over all (Colossians 2:9–10)

The context, background, and meaning of true circumcision (Colossians 2:11–13)

How the death and resurrection of Jesus free us from human traditions (Colossians 2:13–14)

The stability of being rooted, built up, and strengthened in Christ (Colossians 2:2:6–7)

Navigating the river of life

DISCUSS

Take a few minutes with your group members to discuss what you just watched and explore these concepts in Scripture. Use the following questions to help guide your discussion.

I. What impacted you the most as you watched Jay's teaching?

2. **Read Colossians 2:1–4.** We live with a never-ending flow of social media, traditional media, and content coming our way from every direction. Much of this brings "fine-sounding arguments" that are actually broken gauges that are dangerous if we don't identify and name them for what

they are. What are some potential dangers you could face in your culture, church, family, and life if you ignore these broken gauges?

3. **Read Colossians 2:8.** What are some deceptive philosophies that are increasingly embraced and accepted in the culture today? How can you learn to identify these and resist the temptation to accept or ignore them but actually fight against them?

4. **Read Colossians 2:2–4, 9–10,** and **James 3:13, 17.** How have you seen the wisdom, truth, and presence of Jesus help you turn from the philosophies of the world and walk in ways that honor God? Give a specific example of this change.

5. **Read Colossians 2:11–15.** What has Jesus accomplished through his death on the cross? Share how this spiritual reality impacts *one* of the following:

   ○ How you view yourself . . .
   ○ How you view other believers . . .

- How you view sin . . .
- How you view Jesus . . .
- How you view the spiritual battles you face . . .

6. As you navigate the rapids in this river of life, you need to hear Jesus calling out, "My instructions are not optional!" You also need to discover the strength that comes when you paddle with other believers. What is one way your group members can pray for you, support you, or cheer you as you seek to live rooted, built up, and strong in Jesus?

MEMORIZE

Your memory verses this week are from Colossians 2:6–7:

So then, just as you received Christ Jesus as Lord, continue to live your lives in him, rooted and built up in him, strengthened in the faith as you were taught, and overflowing with thankfulness.

Have everyone recite these verses out loud. Ask for any volunteers who would like to say the verse from memory.

RESPOND

What will you take away from this session? What is one practical next step you can take to help you identify faulty and broken gauges that the world offers and stop using them? What can you do to use the true and unbreakable gauges Jesus offers to guide your life?

PRAY

Close your group time by praying in any of the following directions:

- Thank God for the times you relied on worldly gauges and things blew up, but your heavenly Father still protected and watched over you.
- Ask the Holy Spirit to give you a discerning heart to identify where you have been drawn into worldly philosophies. Confess these and ask for power to reject these and fully embrace the truth and leading of Jesus.
- Pray for courage and diligence to take regular steps that will lead to a life that is rooted in Jesus, built up in faith, and strengthened to follow the Savior.
- Ask for power to paddle as a group through the rough waters of this life.

SESSION TWO

R eflect on the material you have covered in this session by engaging in the following between-session learning resources. Each week, you will begin by reviewing the key verse(s) to memorize for the session. During the next five days, you will have an opportunity to read a portion of Colossians, reflect on what you learn, respond by taking action, journal some of your insights, and pray about what God has taught you. Finally, the last day, you will review the key verse(s) and reflect on what you have learned for the week.

DAY 8

Memorize: Begin this week's personal study by reciting Colossians 2:6–7:

> *So then, just as you received Christ Jesus as Lord, continue to live your lives in him, rooted and built up in him, strengthened in the faith as you were taught, and overflowing with thankfulness.*

Now try to say these verses completely from memory.

Reflect: Living in Christ Jesus is a life-long process. We continue, day by day and year by year, to grow in Christlikeness. This means our intimacy with God and the way our life reflects the Savior increases with time. Think about the three images the apostle Paul uses in this passage. *Rooted.* . . . roots grow deeper and wider with time if a tree has water and space to flourish. *Built up.* . . . a building that will stand for generations begins with blueprints or a plan, then a foundation is set, structure is next, and the process goes on. *Strengthened.* . . . no person becomes strong without exercise, good dietary choices, and a lifestyle conducive to health. All three of these word pictures call us to a process of growth. What are you doing to nurture deep roots, build up your faith, and grow strong in Jesus?

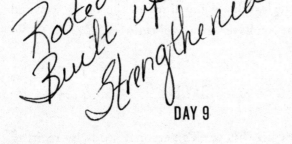

DAY 9

Read: Colossians 2:1–3.

Reflect: The apostle Paul describes the way he ministers and serves Jesus as "contending." He is running hard, working overtime, and pouring out his energy and life for these people. Some of them have never even met Paul. In verse two he describes what he is working so hard to accomplish. Ponder the lofty goals of his ministry for these believers. He longs for them to: 1) be encouraged in heart, 2) be united in love, 3) have complete understanding, 4) know the mystery of God (Christ), and 5) receive all the treasures of Christ's wisdom and knowledge. All five of these are loaded into one verse. How do you fight for Christians you love and care about? What do you long for them to know and experience in Christ?

Journal:
- What are some ways you could encourage the hearts of Christians you know?
- What could you do to walk and live in united love with other believers?

Be examples

Pray: Thank Jesus for the treasures and wonder of his wisdom and knowledge. Ask the Spirit of God to help you go deeper and deeper in his wisdom. If you have tension, conflict, or unforgiveness between you and another Christian, pray for unity and the courage to seek restoration with this person.

DAY 10

Read: Colossians 2:4–5.

Reflect: In these verses we find one warning and two words of encouragement. First, the apostle Paul gave a sober warning that there were people around town who would love to deceive the Colossian believers. Paul knew what the believers in Colossae were facing. There were people who had taken some of the message of Jesus, added a bit of cultural philosophy, sprinkled in a dash of other religions, and mixed up an attractive cocktail that they were serving up around the region. What looked exciting and sounded delicious was actually poison! This Colossian heresy was syncretism and it led people away from Jesus. In an effort to wake up the members of the Colossian church and move them to action, Paul made two bold declarations: he reminded them that they were disciples and they had firm faith in Jesus. This communication between Paul and the believers in the first century echoes through history and speaks to us today. Be disciplined, strong in faith, and don't buy into the modern syncretistic philosophies that sound fine but poison your soul and relationship with Jesus. These words are as needed today as they were more than two thousand years ago. What are some of the dangerous philosophies floating around today that you need to identify, resist, and call others to do the same?

Journal:

- Write down one or two of the false and heretical teachings that exist in the Church today. Why can these be attractive and also dangerously wrong?
- What are some ways you can resist these teachings? How can you encourage others to beware of the poisonous nature of these philosophies?

Become involved in groups.

Pray: Ask God to give you ever-increasing discernment, discipline, and faith in Jesus that helps you resist the deceptive arguments wrapped in false teaching.

DAY 11

Read: Colossians 2:6–8.

Reflect: Thankfulness has fallen on hard times. In a world of social media, we are exposed to the curated and sanitized version of other people's lives and can feel that we don't measure up. We carry around phones that have cameras better than most professional photographers used a decade ago and they have more computing power than a mainframe had just

five decades ago. We feel compelled to get the next upgrade
and are disappointed if we can't. In a time of unparalleled
abundance, we often focus on what we don't have rather than
on all God has graciously provided. What will it take for us
to be genuinely and spontaneously thankful . . . as a lifestyle?
The book of Colossians is emphatic and clear. We need to
grow up in faith. When we are rooted in Jesus, built up in
faith, and strengthened for our journey of spiritual growth,
we will overflow with thankfulness. How thankful are you
today, right now?

What will a lifestyle of thankful look like!

Journal:

- What are some of the things that get in the way of you
  being overflowingly thankful?
- Make a list of who Jesus is and what he has done for you.
  Why should these things fill you with thankfulness?

Pray: Lift up thanks to Jesus for who he is and what he has
done for you. Ask the Spirit of God to make the practice of
thankfulness a growing part of your life.

DAY 12

Read: Colossians 2:9–12.

Reflect: Jesus is fully God and we are made full through a relationship with him. If you are looking for a theological celebration of the divinity of Jesus, look no farther than the book of Colossians. If you are looking for a vision of what a full life in Jesus is like, Colossians paints a vivid picture of this as well. This study of Colossians, called *One Jesus, One People*, is a celebration of who Jesus is and who we become as we follow the Savior. The more you recognize the divine nature of Jesus and the more you grow to love him, the fuller you will be as a person in every aspect of your life. What is the connection between who Jesus is and who we become as we seek him and his kingdom above all?

Journal:

- As you read Colossians, how has your vision and understanding of Jesus expanded?
- How has walking with Jesus given you a full life and made you more of who God designed you to be?

Shadow + Stuff to pointing God

Pray: Lift up praise to Jesus for being Lord of all, the King of kings, and God with us.

DAY 13

Read: Colossians 2:13–15.

Reflect: Dead man walking! Dead woman walking! Jesus is in the business of resurrection now and for eternity. Think about it. We are already living in the resurrection power of Jesus, the Messiah. While we were dead in our sins and utterly powerless to save ourselves or anyone else, God made us alive in and with Jesus. He cleansed us from sin, cancelled our debt, and broke the back of the spiritual forces that held us captive. One day this life will end and we will see Jesus face-to-face. But we walk in the reality and glory of Christ's resurrection right now. We who were dead are filled with life and move through this world animated and alive in the power of the cross and empty tomb. Do you live each day profoundly aware that the life of Jesus courses through your veins and you walk in the infinite victory of your Savior?

Journal:
- Who were you before you received the grace and life of Jesus? How have you changed?
- What did Jesus do to give you life now and for eternity? What can you do to lift up praise and honor to the One who saved you?

Pray: Give praise to Jesus for his sacrifice on the cross, his victory over the spiritual forces of darkness, and for sharing his triumph with you.

DAY 14

Memorize: Conclude this week's personal study by again reciting Colossians 2:6–7:

So then, just as you received Christ Jesus as Lord, continue to live your lives in him, rooted and built up in him, strengthened in the faith as you were taught, and overflowing with thankfulness.

Now try to say these verses completely from memory.

Reflect: One of the results of a life growing in faith is a thankful heart. When we are growing deep roots, building up our faith, and strengthening our relationship with the Savior, thankfulness will well up in our heart and overflow in words and actions. What are some of the things you are thankful for right now? How can you express this overflowing spirit of appreciation and gratefulness? Consider writing a handwritten note, text, or send an email expressing your thankfulness to someone in your life who has helped you grow in your faith.

A GREATER REALITY

COLOSSIANS 2:16–23

Many people, all around the world, have experienced religion. Countless people go to church and take part in worship services. Devout adherents to many expressions of Christianity argue that their version is the best. But all of this fades away like morning mist when a person encounters the living, risen, glorious Jesus! The reality of Christ the Messiah makes everything else seem like a faint, shadowy imitation.

WELCOME

Maria and Marcus, a couple you know, invite you over for dinner. "Do you like Italian food?" they ask. You reply that you do and mention a local eatery you enjoy. Maria says, "Great, when you come over, I will make you my grandmother's Sicilian red sauce recipe. You will love it." A week later, you sit back after a feast with Marcus and Maria and say, "I have to be honest, until tonight I never really had great Italian red sauce over pasta. This was the real deal!"

Some friends are taking a trip to the Grand Canyon. They ask, "Have you ever been there?" You jokingly say, "I've seen pictures and one big hole in the ground looks like another!" They try to convince you that no picture ever taken of the Grand Canyon does justice to the sheer awe and grandeur of standing there and gazing at what is widely considered one of the seven wonders of the natural world. Five years later, while driving cross country, you realize that you can take an hour detour and grab a quick peek and see what everyone is so impressed by. As you stand there, transfixed, sensing the presence of God's power and the breathtaking site before your eyes, you finally get it!

You grew up as a kid in the flatlands of the Midwest and got to be pretty good at snow skiing on a local hill. . . . not a mountain. Your youth group is taking a ski trip to Colorado. You assure everyone that you are a "great skier." When the "Imperial Express Super Chair" drops you off at the top of a Black Diamond ski run at 12,840 feet at the top of Breckenridge Peak 8 you realize, you have never *really* skied before!

In this life, we have all had moments when we thought we had experienced the real thing. But then, in a moment, our eyes were opened and we realized that we had only tasted a sample, felt a fraction, seen a shadow. When we see, feel, taste, and encounter the real, everything changes!

SHARE

Tell about a time you had a wake-up call and discovered that what you had understood or experienced was simply a shadow compared to the glory of what you now comprehended.

WATCH

Watch the video segment for session three. (Play the DVD or see the instructions on the inside front cover on how to access the sessions through streaming.) As you watch, use the following outline to record any thoughts or concepts that stand out to you.

The allegory of the cave

All religious systems and practices are a shadow compared to the reality of Jesus (Colossians 2:16–17)

Putting religious traditions in their right place (Hebrews 10:1; Matthew 5:17)

A lesson from a devoted mother

Asceticism, false humility, bogus visions and the reality of Jesus
(Colossians 2:18)

Ancient problems are often modern problems too
(1 Corinthians 3:16)

Jesus is the head of the body (Colossians 2:19–20)

Jesus is the true foundation (Ephesians 2:19–22)

DISCUSS

Take a few minutes with your group members to discuss what you just watched and explore these concepts in Scripture. Use the following questions to help guide your discussion.

1. What impacted you the most as you watched Jay's teaching?

2. **Read Colossians 2:13–17.** The apostle Paul refers to dietary restrictions, religious festivals, New Moons, Sabbath days, and other things as "shadows" compared to the reality of the risen and glorious Jesus. How can religious actions and observances point you to Jesus in a meaningful way? How is encountering Jesus so much more powerful?

3. **Read Colossians 2:18–19.** There are some teachers who proclaim that in order to have the deepest connection with Jesus, you have to have specific religious experiences. They can give you the impression that if you do *not* have ecstatic encounters with God, overtly "supernatural" stories, or miraculous occurrences in your life, you are second-class members of God's family. What are the dangers of believing this kind of teaching or pressuring others to feel they need to "measure up"?

4. **Read Colossians 2:20–23.** How does the apostle Paul uncover and expose the dangers of religious legalism in this passage? What are ways you can reject modern church legalism and regulations and embrace Jesus as the center of your faith?

5. **Read Ephesians 2:19–22.** It is all about foundations! What are practical ways you can build your life on the foundation of Jesus rather than on human religious expectations? Share one action, attitude, or spiritual discipline that helps you keep your eyes and heart focused on Jesus as your foundation and cornerstone.

Pray - friends

6. As you journey with Jesus and grow in faith, you will do this best in community with the people of God. As you heard in this week's teaching, "When Christ is your foundation and cornerstone, the substance on which you build your life, foreigners become citizens, strangers become family, and old boundary lines of cultural norms of traditions and rituals are redrawn and expanded." How can a true and deep encounter with the living Christ transform your relationships with other believers, with enemies, and with people outside of God's family? Share how you have experienced this.

MEMORIZE

Your memory verse this week is from Colossians 2:17:

These are a shadow of the things that were to come; the reality, however, is found in Christ.

Have everyone recite this verse out loud. Ask for any volunteers who would like to say the verse from memory.

RESPOND

What will you take away from this session? What is one practical next step you can take to move your eyes and focus more directly on Jesus and avoid focusing too much on the practices and structures of religion that are meant to draw us to Jesus?

PRAY

Close your group time by praying in any of the following directions:

- Ask God to help you recognize where you have been leaning into religious practices but not following them to the intended goal. . . . intimacy with Jesus.
- Pray for those who lead your church, children's programs, youth group, worship services, and all that happens in your home church. Ask God to help them lead in ways that allow people to encounter Jesus in a deep and personal way and not just attend church events.
- Take a moment for silent prayer. Confess to God where you have been going through the motions and where your faith has become a shadowy focus on religious observance rather than a deep and personal encounter with your Savior.
- Lift up prayers of thanks and praise for the reality, glory, and goodness of Jesus, the head of the body, the One who is real and shows us what reality truly is!

SESSION THREE

Reflect on the material you have covered in this session by engaging in the following between-session learning resources. Each week, you will begin by reviewing the key verse(s) to memorize for the session. During the next five days, you will have an opportunity to read a portion of Colossians, reflect on what you learn, respond by taking action, journal some of your insights, and pray about what God has taught you. Finally, the last day, you will review the key verse(s) and reflect on what you have learned for the week.

DAY 15

Memorize: Begin this week's personal study by reciting Colossians 2:17:

> These are a shadow of the things that were to come; the reality, however, is found in Christ.

Now try to say this verse completely from memory.

Reflect: Shadows have no substance. We can see them on the ground, on a wall, or anywhere when the sun is shining. Shadows give us a muted picture of something real. They cause us to look and identify what is creating this shadow. The apostle Paul is clear that we can see shadows that point us to things to come. We experience many religious observances and practices, but they are meant to point us to something bigger, better, real! Reflect on some of the things you have experienced that helped you turn your gaze upward toward Jesus and then encounter something greater than the shadow you first saw.

DAY 16

Read: Colossians 2:16–17.

Reflect: Don't let others judge you because of shadowy religious practices and rituals. This is Paul's warning because he understands the human tendency to judge others (even Christians with other believers). This exhortation of Paul can also call us to be careful not to judge other believers on how they adhere to all the ancient or modern legalism and expectations we often place on each other. In addition, we can hear Paul warning us not to judge ourselves on the human rules and regulations we set up in our unique church traditions.

It is so easy to be judged, to judge others, or to condemn ourselves for failing to measure up to all of the man-made do's and don'ts of our particular brand of Christianity. Think about the potential danger and harm that can come if we spend our time and energy judging each other and ourselves on religious legalism.

Journal:
- What are some of the points of religious judgment that take place in your church or faith community (maybe even denominational distinctives that lead to judgment)?
- How do you feel judged by others? How do you judge yourself? How are you tempted to judge other believers?

Pray: Confess where you have been heaping ungodly judgment on other believers or on yourself. Ask God to help you focus on Jesus and the core of the faith and not on human legalism that discourages and divides us.

DAY 17

Read: Colossians 2:18.

Reflect: Beware of puffed-up spiritual pride! We can all be tempted to become religious braggers and spiritual show-offs. Some people do this in overt ways and others are very subtle and sly. But, when we encounter God, are growing in faith, and experience the glorious reality of Jesus, the enemy of our souls wants to corrupt our faith by enticing us to act in pride, arrogance, and spiritual superiority. We need to notice and resist this temptation. When we have a genuine and powerful encounter with the Savior, it should lead to genuine humility and graciousness toward others. How do you respond when God moves in your life in a big way?

Journal:
- Why do you think the devil loves to get Christians to act pridefully and arrogantly when it comes to encounters with Jesus? Why is this so damaging for us and others?
- What are ways you can grow in humility and resist pride when it comes to your relationship with Jesus?

Pray: Invite the Holy Spirit of God to grow you in humility and to protect you from puffed up pride when it comes to your relationship with Jesus.

DAY 18

Read: Colossians 2:19.

Reflect: Stay connected to Jesus, the head of the body. Paul laments the fact that many people had become disconnected from Jesus *while* they were growing in "spirituality." Yes, this happens. We can be very religious, devoted to church-directed practices, and look quite spiritual and still be wandering far from our Lord. As we lose connection with Jesus, the head, we tend to wander farther from the community of God's people, his body. Satan loves this! Jesus grieves over it. We need to do all we can to stay connected to Jesus and his family. Are there ways you are growing away from the Church and the Lord of the Church?

Journal:
- What are ways the enemy seeks to pull you away from connection to Jesus? How can you resist this?

- How do you see yourself enticed to disconnect from the Church, the family of God? How can you battle against these temptations?

Pray: Pray for eyes to see where the enemy is seeking to pull you away from connection in the church and intimacy with Jesus. Ask for power to resist these enticements.

DAY 19

Read: Colossians 2:20–21.

Reflect: What guides your life; human rules and regulations, or the wisdom and leading of the Holy Spirit? Many people are possessed by a spirit of legalism and they are imprisoned by religious shackles. Jesus died to destroy all bondage and set us free! When we receive the Savior's grace and are buried in his death, we experience the power of his resurrection and willingly surrender to his leading, his will, and his truth. Human religious regulations fall to the ground as Jesus is lifted up. Do you feel the freedom of Jesus as you walk through each day as his child?

Journal:
- What are some of the human commands, teachings, rules, and regulations that you still feel pressured to follow?
- What could your life look like if you recognized that you have died with Christ to the influence of these things and are free to follow Jesus out of love, desire, and in joy?

Pray: Thank Jesus for the spiritual reality that you have died with Christ and are raised again in freedom, power, and hope.

DAY 20

Read: Colossians 2:22–23.

Reflect: Human rules and legalism have no power to set us free from the grip of the devil and his demonic strongholds. The divine presence of Jesus and the power of his Holy Spirit in us can set every believer free from the sensual enticements we face. Jesus wants his children to be restrained when it comes to sensual temptations. This will happen when we hold to Jesus, walk in his power, experience his freedom, and see the Holy Spirit unleashed in our thoughts and actions. Where do you look when you need power to follow Jesus and reject the ways of the world?

Journal:
- How do you feel the power of Jesus unleashed in your life when you are set free from human rules and focus on his truth and presence in your life?
- What are some of the ways the enemy tries to draw you into sensual indulgences of all sorts?

Pray: Ask God to give you heavenly power to resist and be restrained from worldly indulgence.

DAY 21

Memorize: Conclude this week's personal study by again reciting Colossians 2:17:

> *These are a shadow of the things that were to come; the reality, however, is found in Christ.*

Now try to say this verse completely from memory.

Reflect: Jesus is more real than all the things of this world. He is the divine Word through whom the universe was made. When we recognize that Jesus is our ultimate reality, everything else begins to look like a shadow. The things we thought were so important, tangible, solid, fade into the background and Jesus becomes our all in all! What are things in this world that used to capture your attention in the past and seemed so real and essential . . . but now are a mere shadow of what they were in your life? If there is something that has taken too big of a place in your heart, offer it to Jesus and ask that his presence would fill your deepest needs.

24 月

CONSTANT DISSONANCE

COLOSSIANS 3:1–11

*There is a raging battle in each of us. We all have things
we long for and desires that are not good for us and
do not honor God or enhance our lives. We also have
knowledge and beliefs that lead us to what is good,
right, and delights the heart of our God. In the power of
Jesus, we can put sinful desires and actions to death
and walk in the resurrection life God has for us.*

1.

WELCOME

I know. . . . but!

These words dwell on the lips and in the hearts of every
human being. There are things we know with deep conviction.
But we can end up living in ways diametrically opposed to
what we know is best and what we really want to do.

- Picture a father talking to his teenage son and daughter with a lit cigarette in his hand. "Kids, these things will kill you! Don't start smoking." He pauses to take a long drag and then exhales the smoke. "I love you both and I am begging you, don't start smoking!"
- Imagine a pastor battling diabetes. His congregation is aware of the struggle and many are praying for his health. His doctor has warned him that this is very serious. She has clearly instructed him to increase his exercise and modify his diet. Unfortunately, he has made no significant life changes in his diet or exercise and his health is growing progressively worse.
- Envision a Christian wife who loves her husband and kids, but she also struggles with strong attraction to a male colleague at work. A small group of women who love her and Jesus are praying for her and have given counsel for her to avoid contact with this man. She knows the danger and does not want to compromise her family but continues to sneak off for lunches with him and texts him often to share personal parts of her life and heart.

I know. . . . but! There is a war between what we know is best, true and good. . . . .and what we often do.

SHARE

Tell about a situation (in the past or even right now) where you faced a personal struggle between what you knew was right and what you found yourself wanting to do (that was not the good and right thing). Why do you think these kinds of battles rage in all of us?

WATCH

Watch the video segment for session four. (Play the DVD or see the instructions on the inside front cover on how to access the sessions through streaming.) As you watch, use the following outline to record any thoughts or concepts that stand out to you.

The battle between our longings and desires and what we know and believe (Romans 7:15)

There are some things that absolutely need to be put to death (Colossians 3:5–10)

Understanding and naming sins of exploitation (Colossians 3:5)

Understanding and naming sins of abuse (Colossians 3:8–9)

The costs and danger if we refuse to put these things to death (Colossians 3:6)

Setting our hearts and minds on the things above. . . . a powerful step into putting sin to death (Colossians 3:1–4)

The place and power of Scripture in this battle (Colossians 3:16)

The need for church community as we stand strong against temptation (Colossians 3:16)

DISCUSS

Take a few minutes with your group members to discuss what you just watched and explore these concepts in Scripture. Use the following questions to help guide your discussion.

1. What impacted you the most as you watched Jay's teaching?

2. **Read Colossians 3:5–10.** Why is it essential to admit and name the sins that plague human beings (all of us)? Why is it good that you feel uncomfortable and awkward when you face the reality that sin is real and knocking on the door of every single one of us?

3. **Read Colossians 3:3–5.** What is Paul getting at when he declares that you have "died" and that you are called to put these sinful actions to "death"? We all have habits, patterns, attitudes, and even motives that we know dishonor God and need to be "put down." So why is it often painful and difficult to "put to death" the things you know are not good for you?

4. **Read Colossians 3:5.** If these sins of exploitation are so hurtful to others and clearly damaging, why do so many people persist in these? Why do you think they have become so acceptable in our culture today?

5. **Read Colossians 3:8–9.** If you allow these sins of abuse to become commonplace in your life and society, what are some of the implications and consequences that you will face (or are already seeing)?

6. **Read Colossians 3:16.** What are some ways you can engage with Scripture and fill your heart and mind with the truth of God's Word so that you can battle against sin? How does consistent and rich engagement in the life of God's family, the Church, empower and help you resist the enticements of sin?

MEMORIZE

Your memory verse this week is from Colossians 3:2:

Set your minds on things above, not on earthly things.

Have everyone recite this verse out loud. Ask for any volunteers who would like to say the verse from memory.

RESPOND

What will you take away from this session? What is one practical next step you can take to identify where you are engaging in some kind of behavior or allowing an attitude to dwell in your heart that you know does not please the God you love? How can you walk away from this and begin the process of putting it to death?

PRAY

Close your group time by praying in any of the following directions:

- Ask God to help you recognize and admit where you are living in a way that is contrary to what you know is pleasing to the Lord you love.
- Pray for growing commitment to go deep in the Scriptures and let the message of Christ dwell deeply in you and shape your lifestyle.
- Lift up your church and pray that all of God's people will see the power of gathering to learn, admonishing one another, singing, praying, and being the family of God together.

SESSION FOUR

Reflect on the material you have covered in this session by engaging in the following between-session learning resources. Each week, you will begin by reviewing the key verse(s) to memorize for the session. During the next five days, you will have an opportunity to read a portion of Colossians, reflect on what you learn, respond by taking action, journal some of your insights, and pray about what God has taught you. Finally, the last day, you will review the key verse(s) and reflect on what you have learned for the week.

DAY 22

Memorize: Begin this week's personal study by reciting Colossians 3:2:

> *Set your minds on things above, not on earthly things.*

Now try to say this verse completely from memory.

Reflect: Not only are there "things above" that are heavenly, glorious, and eternal, but we are taught to "set our minds" on these things. This is not a call to pursue ecstatic religious experience. It is not an invitation to forget the needs of this world. It is a clear declaration that there are good, beautiful, true, and life-giving things that God offers his children and the focal point of our lives should be on such things. As a matter of fact, Christians will be of more use to God's mission and work in this world when we learn to fix our eyes on Jesus and the things that are above as we walk each day in this world. Ask yourself, "What are some of the good and heavenly things I can focus on that will inspire, encourage, and empower me to live this life fully and passionately for Jesus?"

DAY 23

Read: Colossians 3:1–2.

Reflect: "I can't help myself. I can't control my thoughts. I just can't keep from fixating on the things of this world!" Many followers of Jesus say things like this. However, God will never call us to do something that is impossible for us to accomplish in his power. It is possible to shift our eyes and minds off the glittering distractions of this world and learn to fix our hearts on Jesus and the things that are above. What tends to get in the way of you thinking about the things that matter most and last forever?

Journal:

- What are some of the good, beautiful, eternal, and God-honoring things that you can focus on and think about as you walk through a normal day on this earth?
- What habits and patterns can you develop that will help you turn your thoughts to Jesus and your eyes toward the things that matter most?

Pray: Ask God to catch your attention as you walk through each day. Pray that the Holy Spirit will draw your eyes and mind to what honors Jesus.

DAY 24

Read: Colossians 3:3–4.

Reflect: We are simultaneously dead and alive! Every follower of Jesus has died to sin, the power of the enemy, and the control of evil. We have been buried with Christ Jesus. An old way of life and past patterns of thinking are in the grave! Yet it is clear that a battle still rages. We have been raised with Christ and walk in the power of his resurrection life. Our journey is to live as those who are dead to sin and alive to God's presence, plans, and mission. In Jesus Christ, we are alive today and forever and we will one day appear with him in all of his glory and victory. Do you live each day aware that you are dead to an old way of life and alive to the will and life of Jesus?

Journal:
- What are some of the things God buried and did away with when you placed your faith in Jesus?
- How does the enemy try to entice you to wander back into old ways of life that have been crucified and buried with Jesus? How can you battle against these lies?

Pray: Ask the Spirit of the living God to empower you to walk daily in the new life you have in Jesus and to leave your old way of life buried.

DAY 25

Read: Colossians 3:5–6.

Reflect: Sometimes we get confused. We think that when we sin, the amazing grace of Jesus covers all the consequences and that sinful actions don't have a price tag. The apostle Paul addresses this topic in the letter to the Romans. Just because God is forgiving, loving and gracious does not give us license to live in disobedience (Romans 6:1–2). After listing a number of sins of exploitation (Colossians 3:5), Paul reminds us that the wrath of God is coming because of such things. Sin always has consequences. If not for us, then for someone else. Ultimately, the sins of Christians had consequences for our Savior. He bore our sins, the punishment, the consequences, the wrath! We should never take sin lightly. What was your contribution to the weight Jesus carried and the wrath he bore on the cross?

Journal:
- What has Jesus done to take your shame, pay your price, and cover your debt?
- What consequences would you have carried (in this life and in eternity) if Jesus had not taken the wrath and judgment you deserved?

Pray: Thank, praise, and adore Jesus for taking all the punishment you deserved. As you do this, pray over and meditate on these words of 2 Corinthians 5:21, *"God made him who had no sin to be sin for us, so that in him we might become the righteousness of God."*

DAY 26

Read: Colossians 3:7–9.

Reflect: You used to. . . . but you still need to! Let's be honest, we are all works in progress. The apostle Paul reminds the Colossian Christians, and us, that Jesus transforms his people. There are things we used to do and ways that we once lived. But now, in Christ, we are different. We have experienced a glorious new life. We are becoming more and more like Jesus. We are not the same people we were before. But the journey is not over, and the battle continues. After Paul commends them for being changed, he calls them to get rid of a whole list of abusive behaviors, words, and attitudes. Changed and still changing! That is the life of a Christian. Do you recognize how God is working in you today?

Journal:
- What are some of the ways Jesus has changed you and the Spirit of God has led you to a new way of life? Celebrate these!
- What are some of the things you still need to get rid of and what steps can you take to continue your journey of becoming more like Jesus?

Pray: Ask Jesus to show you things you need to get rid of and ask for power to live in new ways.

DAY 27

Read: Colossians 3:10–11.

Reflect: Prejudice, division, and human conflict are not some new inventions of our generation. A cursory review of history reveals that human beings naturally tend toward these things. In our natural state, we can become antagonistic enemies with those who are different from us in their thoughts, appearances, and backgrounds. But in the supernatural power of Jesus, unity, love, and acceptance are not only possible but are also the way of our Savior. In this passage, the apostle Paul emphasizes what Jesus taught over and over when he walked on this planet. The most different, divided, and conflicted people can become a united family through the grace, truth, and presence of our Savior. In Jesus all of our seemingly irreconcilable differences disappear. What are some of the dividing lines that are separating people in our world today?

Journal:

- How have you seen Jesus tear down dividing walls between people in your life and in the life of your church?
- What can you do to join Jesus in his work of tearing down the walls that exist in our world that divide and separate people?

Pray: Thank Jesus for uniting very different kinds of people under the shadow of his cross. Ask him to make you a uniter and not a divider.

DAY 28

Memorize: Conclude this week's personal study by again reciting Colossians 3:2:

Set your minds on things above, not on earthly things.

Now try to say this verse completely from memory.

Reflect: There is a radical and dramatic contrast in this passage. Where do we focus? What consumes our thought-life? Where is our mind fixated? The apostle Paul understands the magnetic pull of this world and the temptation to let our eyes and thoughts linger on earthly things. This world is filled with things that scream for our attention. The stuff of this world can create distraction and even addiction. The messages and mantras of our culture can get locked in our thinking, consume our time and eventually direct our actions. We need to be sure our minds are set on the things of God and not on earthly things. What are some of the things in this world (both material and conceptual) that you can be tempted to focus on and even become obsessed with? What can you do to train your mind and eyes to turn away from these things and focus more on things above?

THE RIGHT ATTIRE

COLOSSIANS 3:12–4:1

As we walk through this life, we find ourselves wearing the clothes that feel comfortable and that we like. The same is true of attitudes, outlooks, and actions. We gravitate toward what feels natural to us. When we encounter Jesus and fall in love with the Savior, our old worldview and lifestyle often no longer fit. Like out-of-style clothes, we take them off and put on our new life in Jesus. This process changes every part of our life!

WELCOME

Jim had a way of cutting corners and doing business that was not really honest or even legal at times, but it made him a lot of money. No one at his company pushed back because he was the boss and was really good at generating revenue that helped the bottom line for everyone. Then, something happened. Jim met Jesus and became a Christian. He was not just going to church and punching a religious clock for an hour every Sunday. He was changed from the inside out.

Within a couple of months, Jim shifted his philosophy of business and adjusted a number of his practices that were a bit shady. He apologized to his employees and told them that he would be exercising integrity in his business dealings and not cutting corners. He asked all of them to do the same. In addition, Jim told the staff that they would still be trying to hit their goals and make the financial bottom line, but there would be more to the goals of the company. Serving the customer, being honest, and bringing a great product to the marketplace would be part of their analytics and bottom line, not just dollars and cents.

As employees watched the culture of the company change for the better, they were encouraged. When they saw how Jim was still energetic, but not driven by only money, they were curious. Over time, the culture of the office shifted, and it felt like someone had opened a window and fresh air came blowing through the whole company. When employees and managers told Jim they liked the new philosophy and ethos, he naturally and comfortably told them about how he had become a follower of Jesus and that he could not live and run the business the way he had before.

In addition to the new focus on service, honesty and excellence, the financial bottom line continued to head in the right direction and the company thrived. When people asked why things were going so well with his business, Jim explained that his old worldview and values drove the company before.

Now, the message and leadership of Jesus shaped how he saw himself, his employees, his customers and the reason for having his business. "Following Jesus is changing my marriage, parenting, business practices, friendships, how I spend my free time, and pretty much everything else in my life. It's a process, but I keep trying to set aside my old way of thinking and living and replace it with a life guided by Jesus."

SHARE

Tell about a way that Jesus is calling and helping you to change the way you think or act in one area of your daily life. What truth from God has moved you to seek personal transformation in this area?

WATCH

Watch the video segment for session five. (Play the DVD or see the instructions on the inside front cover on how to access the sessions through streaming.) As you watch, use the following outline to record any thoughts or concepts that stand out to you.

The right attire. . . . it really matters! (Colossians 3:12–14)

Take off what no longer fits who you are (Colossians 3:5–8)

New clothes . . . putting on what fits a follower of Jesus
(Colossians 3:12–14; Galatians 5:22–26)

Living in the peace of Christ changes everything
(Colossians 3:15–17)

Diving deep into the Scriptures brings transformation
(Colossians 3:16)

Worship in the community of God's people helps us on our
journey of growth (Colossians 3:16)

A household code. . . . how following Jesus changes every part of our lives (Colossians 3:18–4:1)

A daily call to clothe ourselves in Christ:

Compassion

Kindness

Humility

Gentleness

Patience

Forgiveness

Love

DISCUSS

Take a few minutes with your group members to discuss what you just watched and explore these concepts in Scripture. Use the following questions to help guide your discussion.

I. What impacted you the most as you watched Jay's teaching?

2. **Read Colossians 3:12–14** and **Galatians 5:22–26**. What are some of the things you are called to put on (ways God wants you to live)? How can putting on those specific characteristics impact your life for the better over time?

3. **Read Colossians 3:15–17.** When you line up your life with the will and ways of God, his peace rules in your heart and shapes your life. As you grow in following God's Word and go deeper in worship among the people of God, how have you experienced the peace of God in growing measure?

4. **Read Colossians 3:12.** We live in a time of growing conflict, division, and fractured relationships. How can taking off your old ways of life and putting on the clothing of Jesus help you find peace with fellow believers? How can you grow one of these characteristics so that you can walk in peace with other believers?

   ○ Compassion
   ○ Kindness
   ○ Humility
   ○ Gentleness
   ○ Patience

5. **Read Colossians 3:18–4:1.** If you read this passage in the context it was written and with humility, you see a vision of love, respect, hard work, and hope in the home and human relationships. How could a home be transformed for the better if the Spirit of Jesus is empowered to live in ways described in this passage?

6. What is one action or attitude that you need to take off because you are seeking to walk closely with Jesus? What do you need to put on in its place and how could this change your life (and the lives of those around you) for the better?

MEMORIZE

Your memory verse this week is from Colossians 3:14:

And over all these virtues put on love, which binds them all together in perfect unity.

Have everyone recite this verse out loud. Ask for any volunteers who would like to say the verse from memory.

RESPOND

What will you take away from this session? What is one practical next step you can take to develop a lifestyle of taking off the old behaviors and patterns of life and putting on the new life you are offered in Christ?

PRAY

Close your group time by praying in any of the following directions:

- Pray for God to grow compassion, kindness, humility, gentleness, and patience in your life in ever-increasing measure.
- Ask the Spirit of God to help you strive for peace in your relationships. Pray for a deep inner commitment to stay unified in Jesus and not let cultural or personal convictions take precedence over the unity we have in Jesus.
- Praise God for his Word (the Bible) and for the gift of the body of Christ (the Church). Pray for diligence in making personal engagement with both of these a high priority in your life.

SESSION FIVE

Reflect on the material you have covered in this session by engaging in the following between-session learning resources. Each week, you will begin by reviewing the key verse(s) to memorize for the session. During the next five days, you will have an opportunity to read a portion of Colossians, reflect on what you learn, respond by taking action, journal some of your insights, and pray about what God has taught you. Finally, the last day, you will review the key verse(s) and reflect on what you have learned for the week.

DAY 29

Memorize: Begin this week's personal study by reciting Colossians 3:14:

> *And over all these virtues put on love, which binds them all together in perfect unity.*

Now try to say this verse completely from memory.

Reflect: In the ancient world, people knew what a capstone did. When an arched doorway was completed, the capstone was set in place at the very top of the arch. It fit perfectly and held all the other stones in place. This is what love does with all of our spiritual practices, character changes, and actions we take as we walk with Jesus through the world. Love holds them all together. Are you growing in your love for Jesus, for his people, and for the world he came to save?

DAY 30

Read: Colossians 3:12–14.

Reflect: When a Christian reads the Bible with an honest and transparent heart, we have to admit that there are some passages that blow our minds and some exhortations that can seem out of our reach (without the powerful intervention of the Spirit of Jesus). When the apostle Paul writes, "Forgive as the Lord forgave you" (Colossians 3:13), this should shake us to the core of our being. Jesus forgave when we were still rebels (Romans 5:8). Jesus' forgiveness covers all our sin and sets us free. Jesus offers forgiveness to all who will receive it. If the call of God to forgive others as Jesus forgives does not feel overwhelming, we might not be getting the message. How do you need to grow in your commitment to extend the forgiveness of Jesus in the power of the Holy Spirit?

Journal:
- Who has wronged you that you have not yet forgiven (or need to forgive at a deeper level, like Jesus)?
- What steps can you take, both in your heart and in your actions, to extend forgiveness to others?

Pray: Take time to pray for the grace of Jesus and his forgiveness to come upon those who have wronged you.

DAY 31

Read: Colossians 3:15–17.

Reflect: Everything a Christian does and says should be bathed in a thankful spirit. In the name of our Savior and Lord, Jesus the Messiah, we can give thanks to God almighty. The apostle Paul has been writing about what to take off and put on so that we can become God's holy people. He continues with a focus on how a home and family can reflect the presence of Jesus. Right in the middle of this Holy Spirit-breathed teaching the apostle declares that all of this should be done in thankfulness. As you grow in Christlikeness, even in the hard times, remain thankful to your Father in heaven. Is thankfulness natural for you or is it something you need to develop in your soul?

Journal:
- How can you thank God for the growth of Christian character in your heart and life?
- How can you thank your heavenly Father for the way he is at work in your home and family?

Pray: Invite the Holy Spirit to grow thankfulness in your heart, life, and on your lips. Linger right now and begin declaring things for which you are thankful (or should be thankful).

DAY 32

Read: Colossians 3:18–19.

Reflect: Two-way mutual love and submission should mark every Christian marriage. When believers buy into cultural lies or church traditions that lead to competition, domination, and antagonism between a husband or wife, the heart of God breaks. The words in this passage were inspired by the Spirit of God and written down by the apostle Paul so that a man and woman in a marriage relationship would have a pathway to peace and health in their home. When a husband is gentle and loving with his wife, it is natural for her to honor his role in the family and walk in partnership with him. This honors God, strengthens families, and impacts the world. Can you envision homes where love, gentleness, respect, and unity mark the relationship between a husband and wife?

Journal:
- What should gentleness and love look like in a Christian home?
- What should humble submission look like in a Christian home?

Pray: Think of some married couples you know who love Jesus and are seeking to build a home that honors the Savior. Use Colossians 3:18–21 as a prayer guide for these families.

DAY 33

Read: Colossians 3:20–21.

Reflect: In a very similar way to his teaching on the marriage relationship in a Christian home, the apostle Paul calls children and parents to mutual respect and love. Remember, Paul is writing to people living in a highly hierarchical culture and time. When we understand what the apostle is writing, we discover he is not advocating mindless hierarchy but giving us a model for unity and peace in a home that is orderly but not oppressive. He was moving the people of God toward a new kind of home filled with the grace and presence of Jesus. Children were to honor their parents and parents were to honor their children. How did you see (or perhaps not see) this two-way honoring in the home where you were raised?

Journal:

- What could it look like when a child honors their parents as Jesus desires?
- What could it look like when a parent honors their children as Jesus desires?

Pray: Lift up your own family (if this applies) and also parents and children in families you care about. Pray for mutual honor to fill each heart and home.

DAY 34

Read: Colossians 3:22–4:1.

Reflect: In the ancient world slavery took on many shapes and forms. Some were slaves in the oppressive and heart-breaking way that most modern people understand slavery. Others were household servants who were seen as part of a family. We will look at this topic in greater detail in session six, but there is a theme the apostle Paul addresses that can speak to believers today. In all of our life and in the workplace, followers of Jesus should do all their work as if it were for Jesus himself.

What drives a Christian is not ultimately about making people happy but honoring the Lord. What a powerful reminder! We should work at our work with all our heart. Do you see your work and labor as an offering to God or a chore for people?

Journal:
- What is your attitude and disposition toward the work you do?
- What could you do to shift your perspective on work closer to the biblical model expressed by the apostle Paul in Colossians 3:23?

Pray: Ask God to help you (and people you care about) to do all your work for the glory of God and as if you were serving Jesus. . . . because ultimately you are.

DAY 35

Memorize: Conclude this week's personal study by again reciting Colossians 3:14:

And over all these virtues put on love, which binds them all together in perfect unity.

Now try to say this verse completely from memory.

Reflect: When our character is being shaped by Jesus. When we are growing in compassion, kindness, humility, gentleness and patience. When love is binding all these things together. Something happens. Unity, perfect unity, begins to grow in our relationships, home, church and even the community where we live. This is something God longs for his people. Just read Jesus' longest recorded prayer in the Gospels (John 17) and you will see God's desire for unity. What is getting in the way of this in your relational world? What can you do to take a next step into the kind of harmony and unity that God longs for you to experience?

GOD ALONE

COLOSSIANS 4:2–18

Who is worthy of our praise and has the power to hear and answer prayer? God alone! Who loves the world so much that he gave his only Son to save sinful rebels? God alone! Who calls ordinary people to share the message of salvation with the world? God alone! Who levels the worldly playing field so all people can have room at the heavenly banquet table? God, and God alone!

WELCOME

Have you ever used the wrong tool to get a job done?

Try using the heel of a shoe to pound a nail and you'll be wishing you had a hammer right away. After a big snowstorm or freezing rain, try scraping snow off your windows with your hand, the edge of a book, or a credit card. You realize, in that moment, that you would pay good money for one of those sharp-edged hard plastic snow scrapers. Maybe you only had a plastic picnic knife and you tried to cut a thick piece of steak . . . oh, what you would do for a great steak knife. You get the picture. The right tool for the right job is a wonderful gift!

As we walk through life, we use whatever tools are at our disposal. When a friendship goes sideways or a work relationship hits a rough patch, we employ whatever relational tools we have. We navigate pain, loss, and hardship with the emotional tools we have learned to use and they often don't seem to get the job done. When big questions come pounding on the shores of our life, we grab for whatever spiritual resources we can find and try to make it through the storm.

Sadly, the tools we have are often inadequate or ineffective. When it comes to much of life, no one has taught us what really helps. We don't know where to find the wisdom, truth, or skills that lead to a flourishing future.

When we meet God through faith in Jesus, we discover that so many of life's questions find their answers in God alone. We learn that wholeness in relationships comes through God alone and the wisdom he gives. The peace and salvation our souls long for is realized in God alone. The way out of our hellish divisions, conflicts, and hatred is found in Jesus who is the divine One.

When we embrace the reality that the answers to our deepest questions come from God alone, we are not being narrow-minded or exclusive. Instead, we are recognizing that the One who designed us and gave us breath is the only being in the universe who can teach us how to live the abundant life he created us to experience.

SHARE

Tell about a time you tried to fix something or get something done with the wrong tool or solution. How much easier would it have been if you had exactly what you needed for the job?

WATCH

Watch the video segment for session six. (Play the DVD or see the instructions on the inside front cover on how to access the sessions through streaming.) As you watch, use the following outline to record any thoughts or concepts that stand out to you.

A powerful example of prayer

Devoted, passionate, pleading prayers (Colossians 4:2)

Prayers for the proclamation of the gospel (Colossians 4:3–5)

A roadmap for sharing the gospel (Colossians 4:5–6)

Salty speech and not angry and bitter words (Colossians 4:6)

A story and lessons about slavery in the first century
(Colossians 4:7–9)

A great reversal (the book of Philemon)

How Jesus levels the playing field (Philemon 15–17)

DISCUSS

Take a few minutes with your group members to discuss what you just watched and explore these concepts in Scripture. Use the following questions to help guide your discussion.

I. What impacted you the most as you watched Jay's teaching?

2. **Read Colossians 4:2.** Share about an example of devoted prayer that you have seen in the life of someone as you were growing up or right now. What have you learned from this person?

3. **Read Colossians 4:3–4** and **Matthew 28:19–20.** What is the connection between prayer and the spread of the gospel around the world and in your neighborhood? How can you pray as a group and as individuals for revival and a great movement of the gospel in your community?

4. **Read Colossians 4:5–6.** Christians can be salty in their speech and graciously cause people to draw near to Jesus and become spiritually curious. They can also spew out words filled with anger, bitterness, and judgment and drive people away from the Savior. What does it sound like when your words are salty and attractive? How can you train your mouth to be salty and not venomous?

5. **Read Colossians 4:7–9.** In light of the culture of the New Testament world and what the Bible actually says about slavery, what would you say to someone who declares, "I can't believe the Bible because it affirms and celebrates slavery"?

6. The apostle Paul flips the script and does a great reversal. He calls himself a "bond servant" (or slave), even though he was a Roman citizen by birth and a free man. He then goes on to refer to Onesimus (a former slave) as a "faithful and dear brother." How does Jesus bring all of us to a level place in the world when we place our faith in him? How should we treat all other followers of Jesus when we realize God's desire for us to be seen as equal and loved children of his?

MEMORIZE

Your memory verse this week is from Colossians 4:2:

Devote yourselves to prayer, being watchful and thankful.

Have everyone recite this verse out loud. Ask for any volunteers who would like to say the verse from memory.

RESPOND

What will you take away from this session? What is one practical next step you can take to pray with greater frequency, focus, and devotion?

PRAY

Close your group time by praying in any of the following directions:

- Ask the Holy Spirit to grow your passion for prayer and to help you see powerful answers to specific supplications you have lifted to the Father through the Son.
- Pray for words that will be gentle, wise, gracious, and seasoned with salt so that God can use you to draw people to the heart of Jesus.
- Thank God for people who have lived as a model of sharing the story and message of Jesus with winsome and gracious words.

SESSION SIX

R eflect on the material you have covered in this session by engaging in the following between-session learning resources. Each week, you will begin by reviewing the key verse(s) to memorize for the session. During the next three days, you will have an opportunity to read a portion of Colossians, reflect on what you learn, respond by taking action, journal some of your insights, and pray about what God has taught you. Finally, the last day, you will review the key verse(s) and reflect on what you have learned for the week.

DAY 36

Memorize: Begin this week's personal study by reciting Colossians 4:2:

Devote yourselves to prayer, being watchful and thankful.

Now try to say this verse completely from memory.

Reflect: Praying through the flow of our day is good and honors God. Prayer should be like breathing. But there are also moments that demand a vigorous, focused, devoted kind of prayer. During these times we get on our knees or flat on our faces. We don't just talk with God; we cry out from the depths of our soul. We relentlessly pound on the door of heaven and soak the ground with tears. Sometimes prayer looks and sounds like a cry of anguish. What are times in your life that drive you to this kind of prayer?

DAY 37

Read: Colossians 4:2–6.

Reflect: Watch your mouth. . . . people are listening. The apostle Paul is bold in calling God's people to make their speech salty as they share the life-changing message of Jesus with others. Grace should mark all of our verbal utterances. We should think and pray ahead of potential encounters so we are ready to answer questions about our faith and why we live the way we do. In our polarized world, the need for Christians to guard their mouths and strive for grace-filled conversations is as important as ever. People are listening, video cameras are rolling, social media is flooded with soundbites of people dropping their guard and saying something inappropriate.

Don't let the enemy of our souls compromise your witness and example because you say something inappropriate in an unguarded moment. What can you do to increase the grace of God in the words you say?

Journal:
- What are some of the situations where you can be tempted to use your words in a way that could shed a poor light on Jesus and compromise your integrity as his follower?
- How can you increase the grace quotient in your speech in the coming week?

Pray: Confess where your words have been thoughtless, grace-less, or unkind to others. Ask for strength and wisdom to speak words that point to Jesus, reflect his grace, and help others understand the authenticity of your faith.

DAY 38

Read: Colossians 4:7–9.

Reflect: In Jesus we live level. Worldly distinctions fade into the background. Cultural divisions are bridged by the presence of our Savior. The chasm of difference is spanned by the infinite love of our heavenly Father. At the foot of the cross, we all bow to Jesus and come in humility. This means there is no room for "Christian superstars." Pastors are called to be servants. Wealthy people share their possessions with those in need. Strangers become family. Outcasts are invited in. We become a body where every part has an important and valuable role. What are ways we can embrace the spiritual reality that in Jesus we live on level ground?

Journal:
- What are some of the ways Christians, churches, and the broader faith community get this wrong and create distinctions between believers in Jesus?
- What are ways you can lift others up who seem to be pushed down in the family of God?

Pray: Thank God for sending his Son Jesus for all of us, with no regard for any of the human distinctions and differences we often notice.

DAY 39

Read: Colossians 4:10–18.

Reflect: People matter. At the end of many of Paul's letters to the churches of the ancient world, he takes time to greet, encourage, or challenge specific people. "Aristarchus says hi!" "Oh, Mark and Justus say hi too." "Epaphras is praying intensely for you!" "Please be sure to tell Nympha and the people in her house-church hello from me." "Encourage Archippus to hang in there and keep serving Jesus and his church." Why would these details be included in the Holy Spirit-breathed Scriptures? Because people matter to God, and they should matter to us. The Church is a gathering of people who have met Jesus and are seeking to follow him. Each name reflects a person and God sent his only Son to give his life for the lives of people. Do you care about people the way God does?

Journal:
- Who are people in the family of God that you love and care about?
- How has God used each one to deepen your faith and inspire you?

Pray: Thank God for people he has placed in your life that have invested in your spiritual growth. Pray for courage to thank these people for their role in your life and ask God to use you to offer similar blessings in the lives of others.

DAY 40

Memorize: Conclude your forty-day personal study by again reciting Colossians 4:2:

Devote yourselves to prayer, being watchful and thankful.

Now try to say this verse completely from memory.

Reflect: Thankfulness can guide all of our prayers. From simple prayers of thanks, to focused declarations of praise, to heartfelt lament, a thankful spirit should guide our prayers. When the apostle Paul, the author of Colossians had been beaten, wrongfully accused, and locked in prison, his thankful spirit became a witness to others in the jail and to the night crew on his cell block (Acts 16). Why is thankfulness a key part of prayer? What prayers of thanks can you lift up right now?

LEADER'S GUIDE

Thank you for your willingness to lead your group through this study! What you have chosen to do is valuable and will make a great difference in the lives of others. The rewards of being a leader are different from those of participating, and we hope that as you lead you will find your own walk with Jesus deepened by this experience.

This study on Colossians in the *40 Days Through the Book* series is built around video content and small-group interaction. As the group leader, think of yourself as the host. Your job is to take care of your guests by managing the behind-the-scenes details so that when everyone arrives, they can enjoy their time together. As the leader, your role is not to answer all the questions or reteach the content—the video and study guide will do that work. Your role is to guide the experience and cultivate your group into a teaching community. This will make it a place for members to process, question, and reflect on the teaching.

Before your first meeting, make sure everyone has a copy of the study guide. This will keep everyone on the same page and help the process run more smoothly. If members are unable to purchase the guide, arrange it so they can share with other members. Giving everyone access to the material will position this study to be as rewarding as possible. Everyone should feel free to write in his or her study guide and bring it to group every week.

SETTING UP THE GROUP

Your group will need to determine how long you want to meet each week so you can plan your time accordingly. Generally, most groups like to meet for either sixty minutes or ninety minutes, so you could use one of the following schedules:

SECTION	60 MINUTES	90 MINUTES
WELCOME (members arrive and get settled)	5 minutes	5 minutes
SHARE (discuss one of the opening questions for the session)	5 minutes	10 minutes
READ (discuss the questions based on the Scripture reading for the session)	5 minutes	10 minutes
WATCH (watch the video teaching material together and take notes)	15 minutes	15 minutes
DISCUSS (discuss the Bible study questions based on the video teaching)	25 minutes	40 minutes
RESPOND/PRAY (reflect on the key insights, pray together, and dismiss)	5 minutes	10 minutes

As the group leader, you will want to create an environment that encourages sharing and learning. A church sanctuary or formal classroom may not be as ideal as a living room, because those locations can feel formal and less intimate. No matter what setting you choose, provide enough comfortable seating for everyone, and, if possible, arrange the seats in a semicircle so everyone can see the video easily. This will make the transition between the video and group conversation more efficient and natural.

Also, try to get to the meeting site early so you can greet participants as they arrive. Simple refreshments create a welcoming atmosphere and can be a wonderful addition to a group study. Try to take food and pet allergies into account to make your guests as comfortable as possible. You may also want to consider offering childcare to couples with children who want to attend. Finally, be sure your media technology is working properly. Managing these details up front will make the rest of your group experience flow smoothly and provide a welcoming space in which to engage the content of this study on the book of Colossians.

STARTING THE GROUP TIME

Once everyone has arrived, it is time to begin the study. Here are some simple tips to make your group time healthy, enjoyable, and effective.

Begin the meeting with a short prayer and remind the group members to put their phones on silent. This is a way to make sure you can all be present with one another and with God. Next, give each person a few minutes to respond to the questions in the "Share" section. This won't require as much time in session one, but beginning in session two, people may need more time to share their insights from their personal studies. Usually, you won't answer the discussion questions yourself, but you should go first with the "Share" questions, answering briefly and with a reasonable amount of transparency.

At the end of session one, invite the group members to complete the "Your 40-Day Journey" for that week. Explain that they can share any insights the following week before the video teaching. Let them know it's not a problem if they can't get to these activities some weeks. It will still be beneficial for them to hear from the other participants in the group.

LEADING THE DISCUSSION TIME

Now that the group is engaged, watch the video and respond with some directed small-group discussion. Encourage the group members to participate in the discussion, but make sure they know this is not mandatory for the group, so as to not make them feel pressured to come up with an answer. As the discussion progresses, follow up with comments such as, "Tell me more about that," or, "Why did you answer that way?" This will allow the group participants to deepen their reflections and invite a meaningful conversation in a nonthreatening way.

Note that you have been given multiple questions to use in each session, and you do not have to use them all or even follow them in order. Feel free to pick and choose questions based on the needs of your group or how the conversation is flowing. Also, don't be afraid of silence. Offering a question and allowing up to thirty seconds of silence is okay. This space allows people to think about how they want to respond and gives them time to do so.

As group leader, you are the boundary keeper for your group. Do not let anyone (yourself included) dominate the group time. Keep an eye out for group members who might be tempted to "attack" folks they disagree with or try to "fix" those having struggles. These kinds of behaviors can derail a group's momentum, so they need to be steered in a different direction. Model active listening and encourage everyone in your group to do the same. This will make your group time a safe space and create a positive community.

The group discussion leads to a closing time of individual reflection and prayer. Encourage the participants to review what they have learned and write down their thoughts in the "Respond" section. Close by taking a few minutes to pray as directed as a group.

Thank you again for taking the time to lead your group. You are making a difference in the lives of others and having an impact on the kingdom of God!

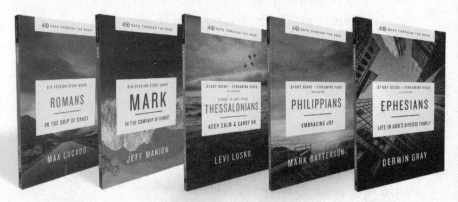